Alaska

• • • • •

Pamela Rushby

Contents

You can see large mountains and lakes in Alaska.

Welcome to Alaska

What do you know about Alaska? Alaska is one of the 50 states in the United States. The name *Alaska* means "great land." The word "great" can mean very large. This is certainly true for Alaska!

Alaska is the largest of all the states in the United States. The next three largest states are Texas, California, and Montana. Imagine putting the land of these three states together. This land would not be as large as Alaska.

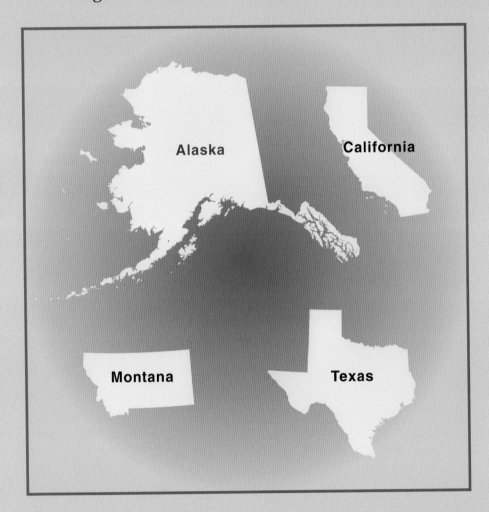

Alaska is much farther north than the other states in the United States. Alaska is located near the **North Pole**. The North Pole is the name of the point farthest north on the Earth.

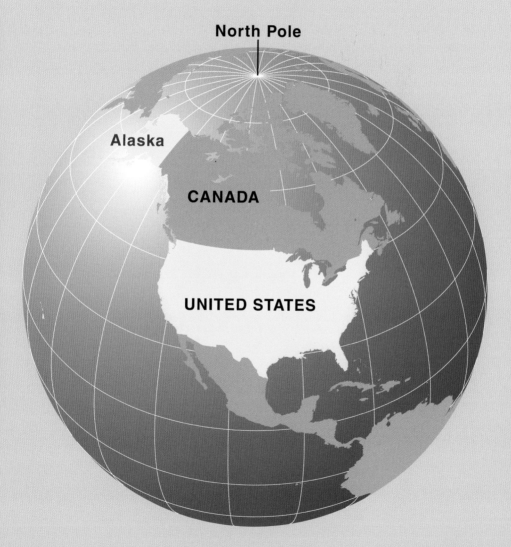

North Pole

Alaska

CANADA

UNITED STATES

Alaska's Weather

Alaska's location near the North Pole means long, cold winters. Heavy snow falls in many parts of the state. Some places have more snow than others. The town of Valdez has about 200 inches of snowfall each winter. That's about 17 feet of snow!

In Anchorage, winter temperatures are around 13 degrees. The farther north you go, the colder it gets. In Barrow, it can be very, very cold in winter. Temperatures fall far below zero.

In the summer, temperatures can be warm. In Anchorage, temperatures can be around 60 degrees. The snow melts in many places.

Barrow.

A l a s k a

Anchorage. .Valdez

Juneau⋆

The ground stays frozen all year in Barrow.

Long Days, Long Nights

Alaska is sometimes called the "Land of the Midnight Sun." That's because the sun does not set until long after midnight during the summer. In the middle of summer, there might be 22 hours of sunlight in a day. Having so many hours of sunlight means Alaskans can play and work outside late into the night during the summer months.

Alaska's location near the North Pole is what causes the days to be so long in the summer. It's also what causes the days to be so short in the winter. During the winter months, Alaskans enjoy only a few hours of sunlight each day. The rest of the day it is dark as night.

The sunlight still shines at midnight in the summer.

Lights in the Sky

Alaska's dark winter sky can be amazing. There are often special lights in the sky called **northern lights**. The northern lights shimmer white, green, and red. These amazing lights happen in the sky in places near the North Pole.

Would you like to see the colorful northern lights?

People of Alaska

Not a lot of people live in Alaska. The **population** of Alaska is very small. There are only about 630,000 people in the whole state. Only the state of Wyoming has fewer people than Alaska.

Alaska has almost 500 times more land than the tiny state of Rhode Island. But Rhode Island has a bigger population than Alaska! This graph shows the populations of some other states compared to Alaska.

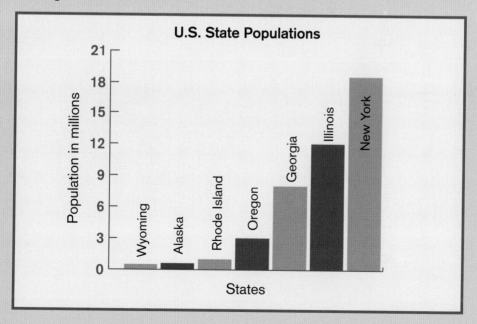

Anchorage, Alaska

Alaska does have some big cities. The population of the city of Anchorage is about 260,000. That is almost half of all of the people living in Alaska! The capital city of Juneau is much smaller. Its population is about 31,000.

Some people live in places that are **remote** and don't have roads leading to them. Roads can be covered with ice and snow in winter, and it's hard to drive a car on them. Many people use airplanes or snow machines to travel from place to place.

People drive snow machines on the snow.

At Work

Some people in Alaska work in schools, banks, and stores just like other places in the United States. Many Alaskans work with Alaska's **natural resources**, such as oil, trees, fish, and land.

People work to bring oil up from the ground to be used for fuel. Others work with **timber**, cutting trees that will be used for wood or paper.

People work to move timber out of the state.

Many Alaskans work in the fishing industry. More fish come from Alaska than from any other state. Alaska's fishing boats pull in more than five billion pounds of seafood each year.

More than one million **tourists**, or people on vacation, visit Alaska every year. That's more people than live in the state! Some Alaskans work at jobs in shops, restaurants, and tour companies.

Do more tourists visit Alaska in summer or winter?

winter tourists
252,600

summer tourists
1,276,200

Alaska's Tourists

A group of people play a game called blanket toss.

Native People

Alaska is home to many **native** people. Natives are the first people to have lived in a place. Groups of native people have been living in Alaska for hundreds of years.

Many Alaskan natives have kept their old **traditions**, or ways of doing things. Parents and grandparents teach things like games, art, and cooking to their children. They learned these traditions from their parents and grandparents, too. Alaskans are proud to still have these traditions today.

Totem poles are carved and painted with animals and people from Alaskan stories.

Alaska: A Big Adventure

There is much to do outdoors in Alaska. In winter Alaskans ski, skate, and play games. People also do something called **mushing**, which means dogsledding! Alaska's state sport is mushing.

One of the year's biggest events is the Iditarod Trail Sled Dog Race. Mushers drive their dogs over 1,049 miles of snowy land. The race takes nine days. Hundreds of people take part in this race held every March.

A mushing team begins the long race in Anchorage, Alaska.

In summer, people make the most of the long hours of daylight. Many explore the **wilderness**, or natural places where few people live. Many of these places are now part of Alaska's **national parks**.

In Denali National Park, you can see North America's tallest mountain, Mount McKinley. Alaskans call this giant mountain Denali, which means "the great one." This mountain is almost four miles high. It is covered with snow and slow-moving rivers of ice, called **glaciers**.

Tourists often see moose in Alaska.

A glacier has formed
on the side of Mount McKinley.

It seems that everything in Alaska is big. Of all the states, Alaska has the tallest mountains, the largest glaciers, and the most land. Alaska even has the most sunshine in the summer. If you're lucky enough to travel in Alaska, you can be sure that it will be a big adventure!

Tourists enjoy riding bikes in Alaska's national parks.

Glossary

glacier   a slow-moving river of ice

mushing   dogsled racing

national park   land set aside for protection and for people to enjoy

native   the first people to have lived in a place

natural resource   something found in nature that is valuable to humans

northern lights   lights in the sky that can be seen near the North Pole

North Pole   the name of the point farthest north on the Earth

population   the number of people living in a place

remote   far from cities and towns

timber   wood that is used for building things

tourist   a person on vacation

tradition   customs and beliefs passed from one generation to another

wilderness   natural places where few people live

Index